Let's Build an Invention

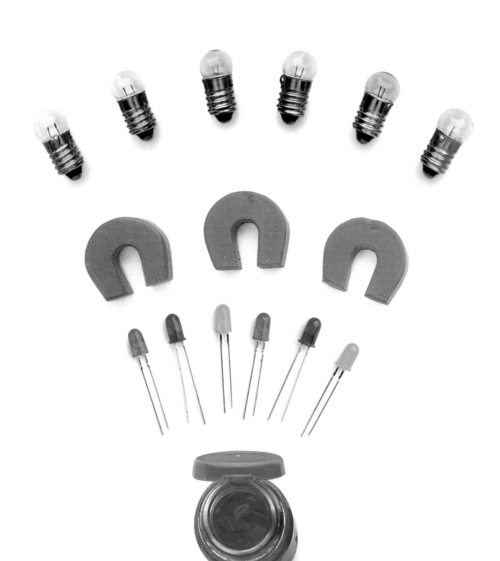

Let's Build
an Invention

JACK CHALLONER, DAVE KING,
and ANGELA WILKES

DORLING KINDERSLEY
London • New York • Stuttgart • Moscow

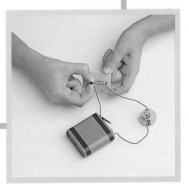

How to use this book

Let's Build an Invention is full of exciting projects to do at home that will help you to find out more about cameras, electricity, and how things work.
Below are the points to look for on each page when using this book, and a list of things to remember.

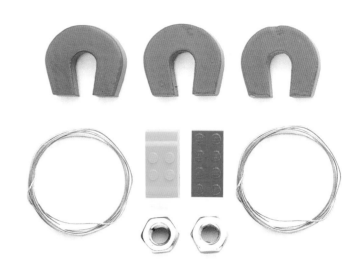

Equipment
Illustrated checklists show you which tools to have ready before you start a project.

The things you need
The items for each project are clearly shown to help you check that you have everything you need.

Step-by-step
Step-by-step instructions tell you exactly what to do at each stage of the project.

Things to remember

- Read all the instructions and gather together everything you will need before you begin a project.

- Be very careful when using wire strippers, scissors, and screwdrivers. Do not use them unless an adult is there to help.

- Always turn off battery-powered projects when you are not using them as batteries may get hot, or run down.

- For projects requiring electricity, always use batteries. Never use electricity from the wall sockets, because it is very dangerous.

- When you have finished, put your project away safely and tidy up everything you have used.

A DORLING KINDERSLEY BOOK

Editor Sarah Johnston
Designers Caroline Potts and Adrienne Hutchinson
DTP Designer Almudena Díaz
Managing Editor Jane Yorke
Managing Art Editor Chris Scollen
Production Ben Smith
Photography Dave King

First published in Great Britain in 1997
by Dorling Kindersley Limited,
9 Henrietta Street,
London WC2E 8PS

A CIP catalogue record for this book is available from the British Library.

ISBN 0-7513-5586-0

Colour reproduction by Colourscan
Printed and bound in Italy by L.E.G.O

CONTENTS

PINHOLE CAMERA   6

CAMERA OBSCURA   8

MAKING
CONNECTIONS   10

STOCK CARS   12

LIGHTING-UP TIME   14

MOTOR MANIA   16

FAN-TASTIC   18

ELECTROMAGNETS   20

BUSY BUZZER   22

WEATHER STATION   24

WEATHER WATCH   26

MAKE IT MOVE   28

THE FINISHED
ZOETROPE   30

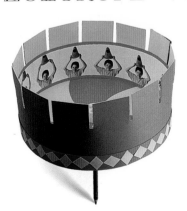

PINHOLE CAMERA

Make a pinhole in a light-proof box, put tracing paper on the opposite side, and instantly you have a simple camera! When light passes through the pinhole, it forms an image on the tracing paper. Find out how on the opposite page. If you used photographic paper (special paper that reacts to light) on the back of the box instead of tracing paper, a photograph would be produced. But, to see the image, you would need a darkroom and developing equipment.

Making the camera

1 Gently take the box apart and paint it. Paint the inside black. Let the box dry. Ask an adult to cut a large rectangle out of one side.

2 Ask an adult to cut a small square out of the side of the box opposite the rectangle. Glue the box back together. Let it dry.

3 Tape tracing paper over the large rectangular hole and foil over the square. Prick the centre of the foil with a pin to make a hole.

You will need

Coloured sticky tape

Tracing paper

Strong glue

Poster paints

Kitchen foil

Small cardboard box with a hinged lid

EQUIPMENT

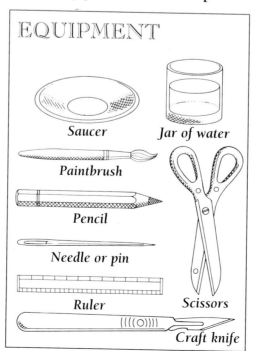

Saucer

Jar of water

Paintbrush

Pencil

Needle or pin

Ruler

Scissors

Craft knife

The finished pinhole camera

It is difficult to make a neat pinhole through card. This is why a piece of kitchen foil is used.

Pinhole

Tape along the box edges. This gives a neat finish and stops light getting into the box.

The box must shut out the light.

Using the camera

Hold the box with the foil at the front.

Point the camera towards a window or an object in bright light. You will see an upside-down image on the tracing paper.

You will see a stronger image if you cover your head and the back of the box with a cloth.

HOW IS THE IMAGE FORMED?

Light travels in straight lines. Every object reflects some light. Here, light is reflected off the girl. It passes through the pinhole on to the tracing paper and forms a picture of the girl. If the pin hole is too big, the light will spread over a large area and form a blurred image.

The brighter the image, the easier it will be to see. Ask a friend to stand near a window so that he or she is brightly lit.

The further away the object is from the pinhole, the smaller the image will be on the tracing paper.

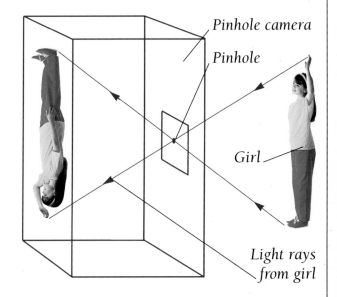

Pinhole camera

Pinhole

Girl

Light rays from girl

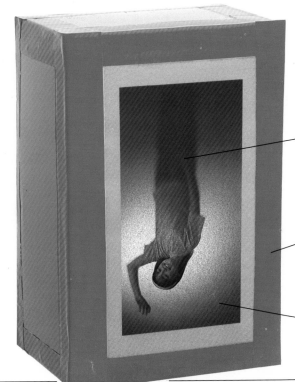

The image of the girl is upside-down and reversed.

Pinhole camera

Tracing paper

WHY IS THE IMAGE UPSIDE-DOWN?

The light coming from the girl's head passes through the pinhole in a downward direction to the bottom of the tracing paper. The light coming from the girl's feet passes through the pinhole in an upward direction to the top of the tracing paper. This happens to light from all over the girl, making the image upside-down and reversed.

Camera Obscura

Instead of a pinhole, this camera uses a magnifying glass to form a picture on tracing paper. The glass works in a similar way to the lens on a "real" camera. It lets in more light than a pinhole, so it gives a brighter image*.

You will need

Card

Tracing paper

Small cardboard box with a hinged lid

Poster paints

Strong glue

Coloured sticky tape

Small magnifying glass, with magnification of about x 2 (You can buy these from stationery shops.)

Making the camera

1 Gently take the box apart and paint it. Paint the inside black. Let the box dry. Ask an adult to cut a large rectangle out of one side.

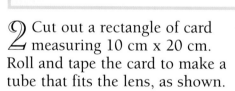

2 Cut out a rectangle of card measuring 10 cm x 20 cm. Roll and tape the card to make a tube that fits the lens, as shown.

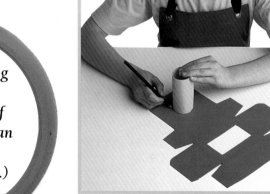

3 Hold the tube on the side of the box that is opposite the large rectangular hole. Draw round it with a pencil.

Unlike the pinhole camera, this camera gives a sharp image with a large hole because the lens focuses the light.

4 Ask an adult to cut out the circle you have drawn with a craft knife. Glue the box back together and leave it to dry.

5 Cut a piece of tracing paper to fit over the rectangular hole on one side of the box. Tape the tracing paper over the hole.

6 Slot the tube into its hole, as shown. You should be able to slide it in and out of the box. Tape the magnifying glass to the tube.

The finished camera obscura

The camera obscura was developed from the pinhole camera. Camera obscuras, similar to the one you have made, were used by artists more than 400 years ago to cast an image on to a wall or canvas, which they would then copy.

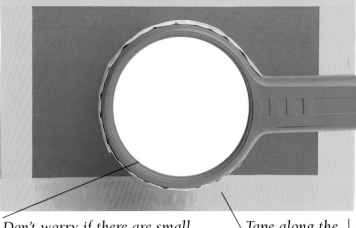

Don't worry if there are small gaps around the tube. The camera will still work.

Tape along the box edges to stop light getting in.

Focus by pushing the tube in or out.

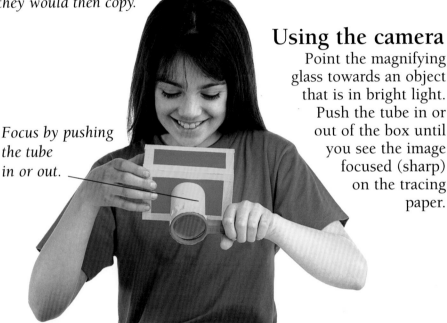

Using the camera

Point the magnifying glass towards an object that is in bright light. Push the tube in or out of the box until you see the image focused (sharp) on the tracing paper.

HOW DOES IT WORK?

Light rays coming from the object pass through the magnifying glass. The glass bends the rays and makes them meet (or focus) on the tracing paper, where they form a picture.

CAMERA LENSES

Camera lenses are more complicated shapes than a magnifying glass and make even sharper pictures. Instead of tracing paper, there is light-sensitive film in a "real" camera. When you take a photograph, an image is formed on the light-sensitive film. The photograph is then developed and printed.

Just like the picture formed by the pinhole camera, the image on the tracing paper is upside-down and reversed.

Camera obscura

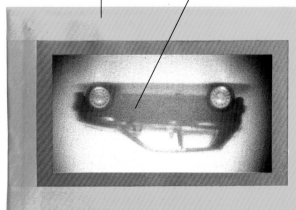

MAKING CONNECTIONS

Batteries can make things happen! They produce electricity, which can turn a motor or light a bulb. Before the electricity can flow, it must have a path from one side, or terminal, of the battery to the other. This path is called a circuit. On this page you will find out how to connect a battery in a circuit, to light a bulb and also make a switch to turn the bulb on and off.

You will need

Wire

A 4.5V battery

A 3.5V or 4.5V bulb

A bulb holder

Paper-fasteners

A steel paper-clip

Making a simple circuit

1 Cut two pieces of wire, and carefully strip about 2 cm of plastic from their ends. Twist the bare metal strands together.

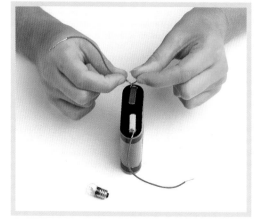

2 Twist a wire tightly around each of the battery terminals, as shown. Make sure that the bare wire is touching the terminal.

Corrugated cardboard

3 Touch one wire to the bottom of the bulb and one to the side. You have made a complete circuit, and the bulb will light up.

4 Screw the bulb into the bulb holder, and attach the wires as shown, using a small screwdriver. The bulb still lights up.

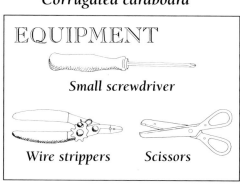

EQUIPMENT

Small screwdriver

Wire strippers   *Scissors*

Making a switch

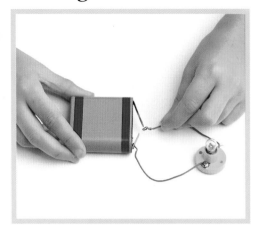

5 Take one of the wires off the battery. The bulb will go out, because there is no longer a complete circuit.

6 Cut another piece of wire. Strip away 2 cm of plastic from each end of the wire and twist the metal strands, as before.

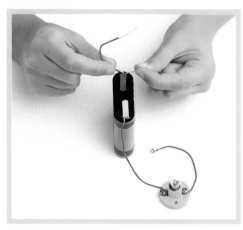

7 Attach one end of the wire to the disconnected terminal of the battery. The other end of the wire will connect to the switch.

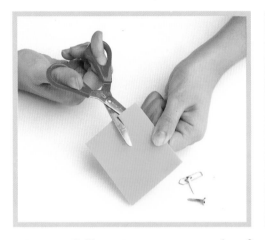

8 Carefully cut out a rectangle of cardboard, about 3 cm x 5 cm. This is the base that will hold the pieces you need for the switch.

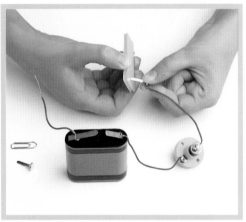

9 Wind the end of the wire from the bulb holder firmly around a paper-fastener and push the fastener through the cardboard.

10 Do the same with the end of the other wire, as shown, but this time put a paper-clip around the paper-fastener as well.

THE COMPLETED CIRCUIT

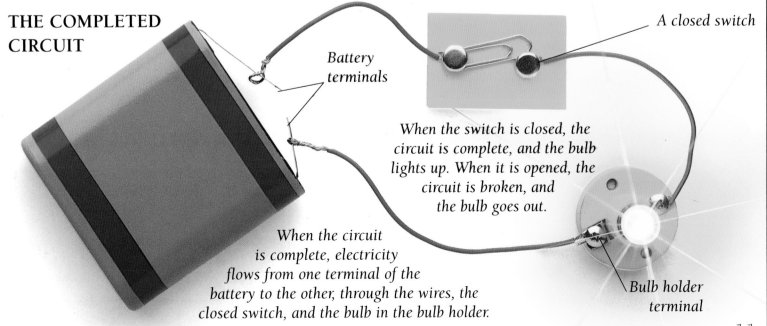

A closed switch

Battery terminals

When the switch is closed, the circuit is complete, and the bulb lights up. When it is opened, the circuit is broken, and the bulb goes out.

When the circuit is complete, electricity flows from one terminal of the battery to the other, through the wires, the closed switch, and the bulb in the bulb holder.

Bulb holder terminal

STOCK CARS

Did you know that a car's lights are powered by a battery? The lights are connected in two different types of circuit. Headlights are connected "in series" (the bulbs are wired together, one after the other, in a circuit). The indicators are connected "in parallel" (two separate circuits are connected to the same battery). Here you can find out how to make a "smashing" stock car with working headlights and indicators.

About 1 m of wire

Four wooden skewers

You will need

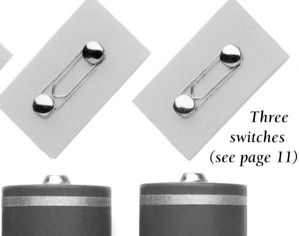

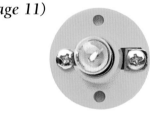

Three switches (see page 11)

Strong glue

Three 1.5V batteries

An egg box

Four 1.5V bulbs in bulb holders

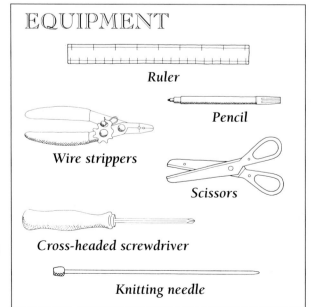

EQUIPMENT

Ruler

Pencil

Wire strippers

Scissors

Cross-headed screwdriver

Knitting needle

A shoe box, with its lid

Coloured card

Four model car wheels, or circles of stiff card

Coloured sticky tape

Kitchen foil

Making the car body

1 Cut away the box, as shown, making sure that the long sides of the car are the same*. Tape the back flap to the sides of the car.

2 Cut down the box lid to fit the top of the car and a windscreen. Fold down the cut end to make the windscreen, and tape it in place**.

3 Push a wheel on to each pair of skewers. Make holes for axles: two holes at the rear of the car and two below the windscreen*.

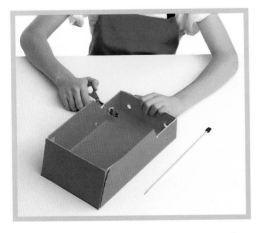

4 Make two holes, large enough for a bulb to go through, in the front of the car. Then, make a hole on either side of the bonnet.

5 Poke the skewers through the axle holes and push wheels on to the ends. Decorate the stock car with pieces of coloured paper.

6 Cover two cups from an egg box with foil. Make a big hole in the bottom of each, then glue one over each headlight hole.

*Ask an adult to help you with this.   **The piece of lid left over becomes the car's bonnet.

13

LIGHTING-UP TIME

Headlights "in series"

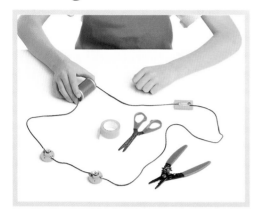

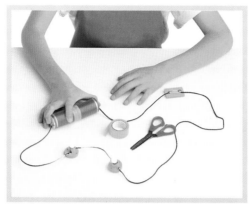

Indicators "in parallel"

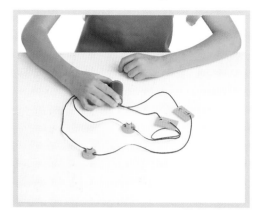

1 Connect two bulbs "in series" in a circuit, as shown. The lights are dim as one battery is too weak to power two bulbs in series.

2 Tape the top of one battery to the bottom of another, in series. Connect the batteries to the circuit, as shown. Now the lights are bright.

3 Connect two separate circuits, each with a bulb and a switch, to one battery, as shown. Bulbs wired "in parallel" shine brightly.

Stock car smash-up

The car headlights are wired in series because both lights need to be on at the same time. Indicators are used one at a time, so they are wired in parallel, with separate switches.

Glue a large paper number to the roof, sides, and bonnet of your stock car.

BRIGHT LIGHTS!

Foil cups around the headlights reflect the light forward from the bulbs. This makes the headlights appear brighter.

Fitting the lights

1 Put the headlights circuit into the car. Glue the switch to the back of the car. Push one bulb through each foil cup, as shown.

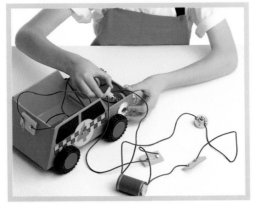

2 Glue a foil-covered card circle over both side holes. Make a big hole in each, as before. Push an indicator bulb through each hole.

3 Put the circuit in the car. Glue the left indicator switch to the left side of the car and the right indicator switch to the right side.

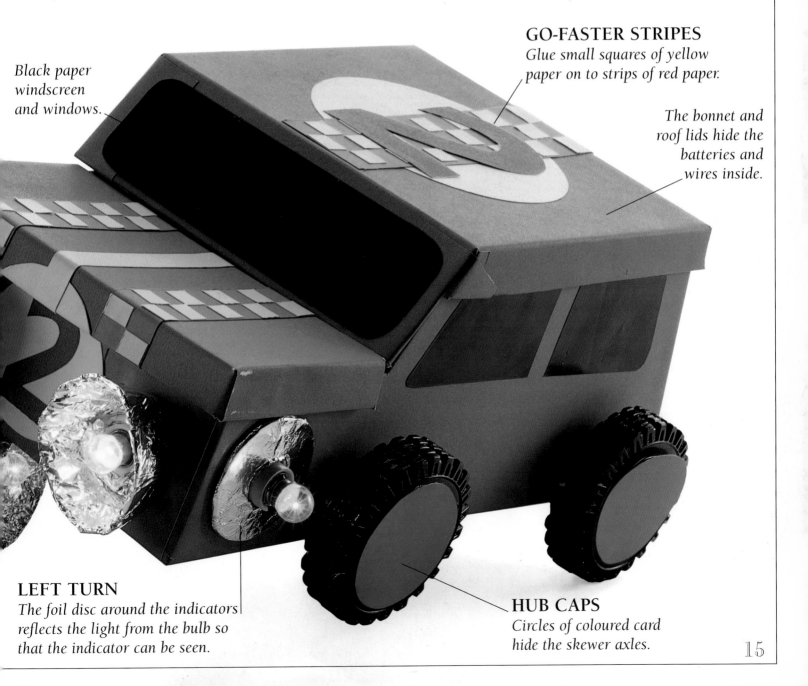

Black paper windscreen and windows.

GO-FASTER STRIPES
Glue small squares of yellow paper on to strips of red paper.

The bonnet and roof lids hide the batteries and wires inside.

LEFT TURN
The foil disc around the indicators reflects the light from the bulb so that the indicator can be seen.

HUB CAPS
Circles of coloured card hide the skewer axles.

15

MOTOR MANIA

Electricity can do a lot more than light bulbs. If you connect a battery to an electric motor, you can make things move too! Here, and on the next two pages, you can find out how to make colourful fans to keep you cool, and a spectacular, whirling merry-go-round.

Cotton buds

Pipe-cleaners

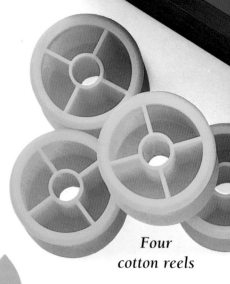

Four cotton reels

You will need

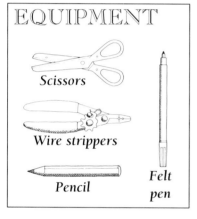

EQUIPMENT

Scissors

Wire strippers

Pencil

Felt pen

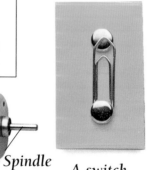

Pattern for the vultures

A switch (see page 11)

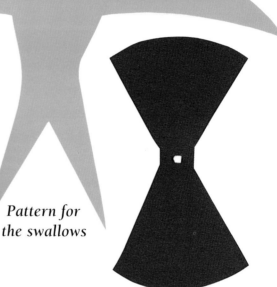

Pattern for the swallows

Pattern for the fans

Motor terminals

A 1.5V-4V electric motor Spindle

A 1.5V battery

Connecting the motor

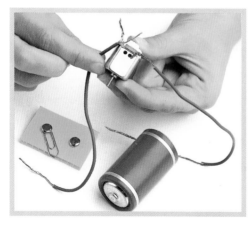

1 Connect a stripped wire to each terminal of the motor, as shown*. Cut a stem from a cotton bud. Push it on to the spindle.

2 Connect motor in a circuit, as shown. Glue the motor to the box, so that the top of the spindle is level with the top of the box.

3 To make a "sleeve", roll a strip of paper around the knitting needle. The sleeve must fit snugly into the centre of one cotton reel.

* Divide the end of the wire in half, thread one half through the terminal, then twist the two halves together.

A small
cardboard box

1 m
of wire

Coloured
paper

Coloured
felt

Sticky tape

A big and small rubber band

Modelling clay

Glue

A knitting needle

Making the merry-go-round

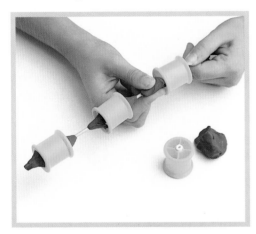

4 Stick the three other reels in place on the needle with the clay, as shown. Glue the reel with a sleeve to the bottom of the box.

5 Stretch the big rubber band on to the box. Put the small band on to the reel that is third from the top of the needle, as shown.

6 Use three pipe-cleaners for each bird – one for the head and body, and one for each wing. Bend vultures' heads, as shown.

7 Trace the vulture and swallow patterns, then cut them out in coloured felt. Stick the birds to the six pipe-cleaner bodies with tape.

8 Tape a pipe-cleaner to each bird, then tape all the birds to the top two reels, as shown. Stand the needle in the reel, in the box.

9 Glue a ring of card to the top reel. Stretch the small band on to the spindle. Make sure the tops of the motor and reel are level**.

*Adjust the cotton reel with the band on it as necessary.

FAN-TASTIC

Making a fan

1 Use the pattern on page 16 to cut out a card fan. Make a hole in the middle of it with a pencil. Decorate it with coloured paper.

2 Connect a switch, motor, and battery together in a circuit. Push a tube cut from the stem of a cotton bud on to the motor.

3 Push the fan shape on to the spindle. Stick it in place with modelling clay. Bend the card up, as shown, to make the fan blades.

WHIRLING MERRY-GO-ROUND

Add the finishing touches to your merry-go-round by putting the battery in one corner of the box, where it won't be seen. Then, glue the switch to the outside, where you can turn it on and off easily.

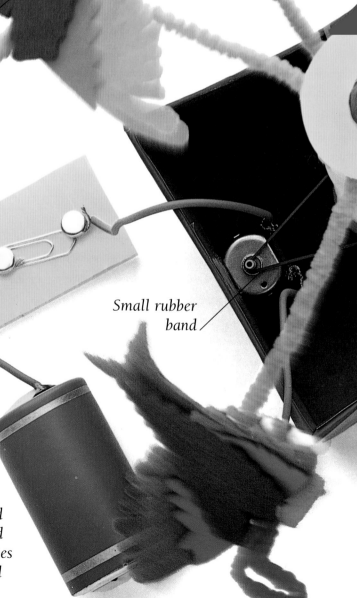

Blue felt swallow

Pink, blue, and yellow felt vulture

Pipe-cleaner supports

Small rubber band

IN A SPIN

As the motor runs, the spindle turns very quickly, making the small rubber band stretched between the needle and the spindle move round too. This, in turn, makes the knitting needle and merry-go-round spin.

COOL IT!

The folded blades of the fan push the air out of the way as they whizz round, producing a lovely, cooling breeze.

Pink and blue felt vulture

ADJUSTER

Adjust the big rubber band around the box to keep the knitting needle vertical. This will stop the small rubber band slipping off the motor.

FAN FUN

Now you have made your fan, you can start experimenting with it. Find out what happens if you connect the battery the other way round in the circuit. Try folding the blades up in the other direction. What happens to the amount of breeze the fan produces?

Big rubber band

Experiment by decorating fan blades with different colours and patterns, then watch how they change as the fans spin round.

19

ELECTROMAGNETS

You can make magnets with electricity, too. They are called electromagnets and, unlike ordinary magnets, their magnetic powers can be switched on and off. All you need is a battery, some wire, a screwdriver, and a switch. The experiment works best if the screwdriver has an iron shaft, but a steel shaft will do.

Sticky tape

You will need

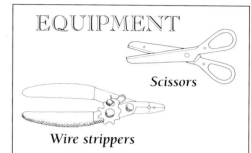
About 2 m of wire

EQUIPMENT
Scissors

Wire strippers

A switch (see page 11)

A 4.5V battery

Lots of paper-clips

A long screwdriver

What to do

1 Strip the ends of a long piece of wire. Tape one end to the handle of a screwdriver, leaving the other end of the wire free.

2 Wind the wire tightly around the screwdriver 20, 40, or 60 times. Tape the last turn of the wire firmly to the screwdriver.

3 Connect the switch, battery, and screwdriver in a circuit, as shown. How many paper-clips can each electromagnet pick up?

20

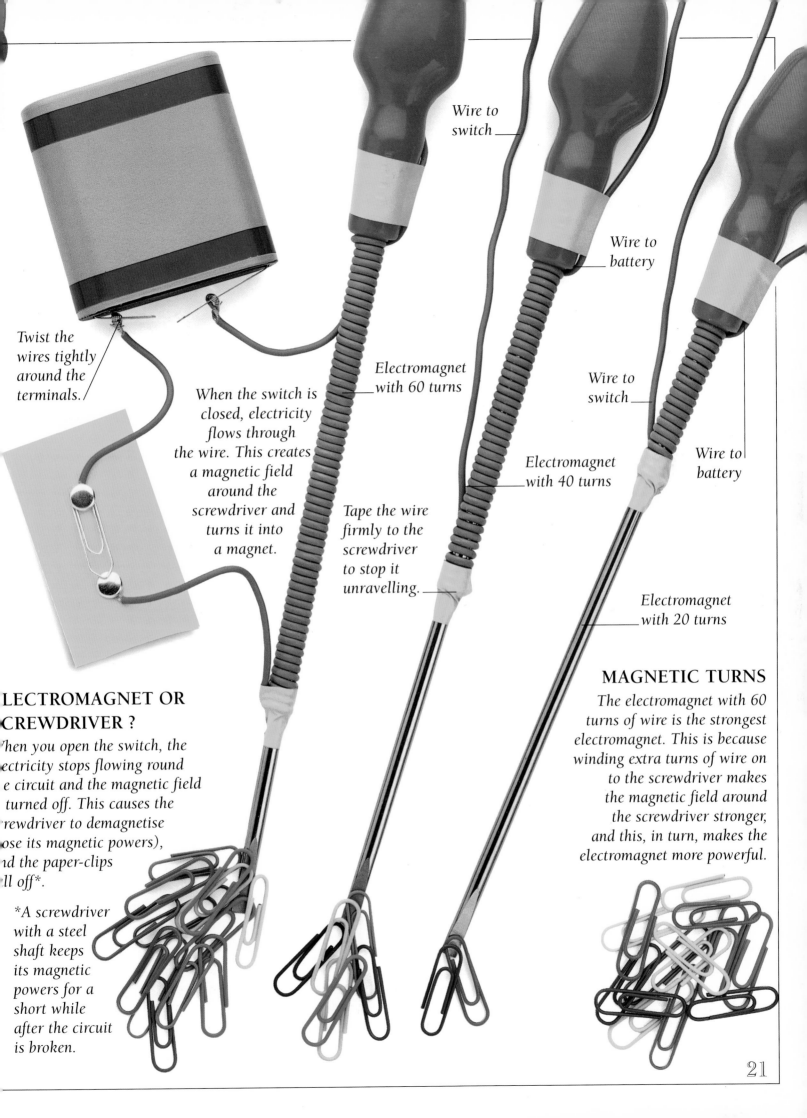

Twist the wires tightly around the terminals.

Wire to switch

Wire to battery

Wire to switch

Wire to battery

When the switch is closed, electricity flows through the wire. This creates a magnetic field around the screwdriver and turns it into a magnet.

Electromagnet with 60 turns

Electromagnet with 40 turns

Electromagnet with 20 turns

Tape the wire firmly to the screwdriver to stop it unravelling.

ELECTROMAGNET OR SCREWDRIVER ?

When you open the switch, the electricity stops flowing round the circuit and the magnetic field is turned off. This causes the screwdriver to demagnetise (lose its magnetic powers), and the paper-clips fall off*.

*A screwdriver with a steel shaft keeps its magnetic powers for a short while after the circuit is broken.

MAGNETIC TURNS

The electromagnet with 60 turns of wire is the strongest electromagnet. This is because winding extra turns of wire on to the screwdriver makes the magnetic field around the screwdriver stronger, and this, in turn, makes the electromagnet more powerful.

21

BUSY BUZZER

You will need

Once you know how to make an electromagnet (see page 20), you can build this noisy buzzer. The handle of the nail-file and the paint on the drinks can don't conduct electricity, so make sure that wires are only connected to bare metal, or the buzzer won't work. Look at the photograph of the buzzer circuit, to check that you have put everything in the right place.

A 4.5V battery

A metal drinks can

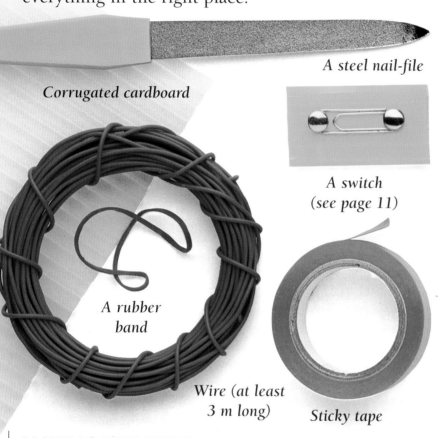
Corrugated cardboard

A steel nail-file

A switch (see page 11)

Modelling clay

A cotton reel

A rubber band

Wire (at least 3 m long)

Sticky tape

An iron or steel bolt

A switch (see page 11)

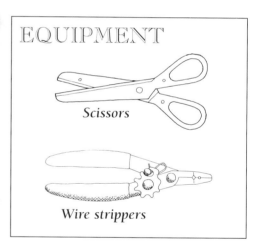
EQUIPMENT

Scissors

Wire strippers

MAKING THE BUZZER

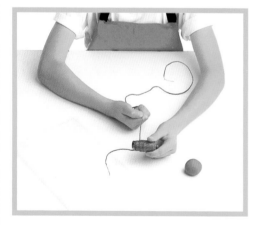

1 Wrap the wire firmly around the bolt 200 times. Strip both ends of the wire. Stick the bolt to the cardboard with modelling clay.

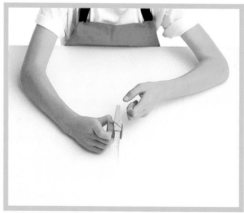

2 Attach the nail-file to the cotton reel with the rubber band, as shown. Make sure that the nail file is held tightly in place.

3 Use the scissors to scratch away two squares of paint, along the bottom edge, on opposite sides of the drinks can.

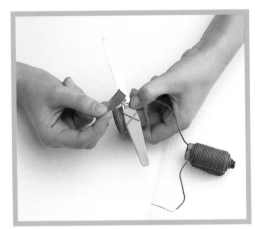

4 Firmly tape a wire from the bolt to the metal part of the nail-file, as shown. Stick the cotton reel in place on the card with clay.

5 Cut a short piece of wire and strip its ends. Attach one end to the battery. Tape the other to one of the scratched squares on the can.

6 Stick the can to the card with clay, so that the other square touches the nail-file. Connect the bolt to a switch, then to the battery.

BUZZING ABOUT

When you close the switch, electricity flows around the circuit. The bolt becomes an electromagnet and pulls the nail-file away from the can. This breaks the circuit, so that the electromagnet loses its power and the nail-file springs back, hits the can, and completes the circuit again. This process happens over and over, very quickly.

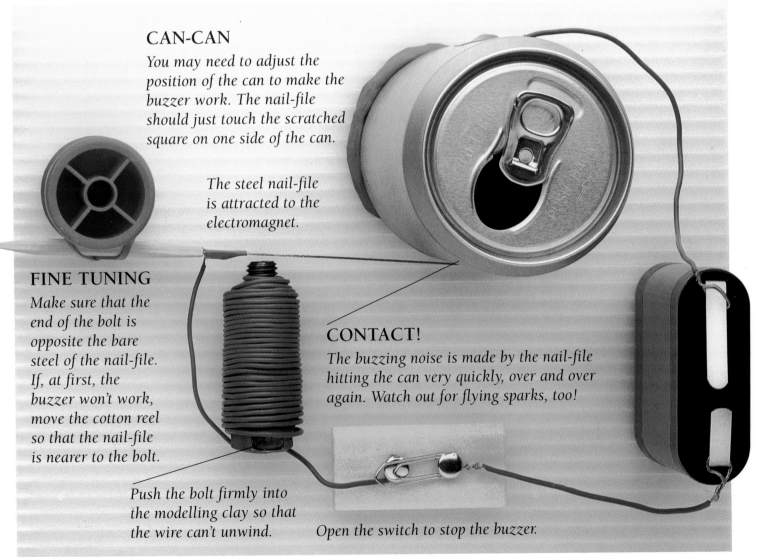

CAN-CAN

You may need to adjust the position of the can to make the buzzer work. The nail-file should just touch the scratched square on one side of the can.

The steel nail-file is attracted to the electromagnet.

FINE TUNING

Make sure that the end of the bolt is opposite the bare steel of the nail-file. If, at first, the buzzer won't work, move the cotton reel so that the nail-file is nearer to the bolt.

Push the bolt firmly into the modelling clay so that the wire can't unwind.

CONTACT!

The buzzing noise is made by the nail-file hitting the can very quickly, over and over again. Watch out for flying sparks, too!

Open the switch to stop the buzzer.

WEATHER STATION

Set up your own weather station and you will be able to keep a record of your local weather. Here and overleaf you can find out how to make a rain gauge, for measuring rainfall, a barometer, to show changes in the air pressure, and a wind vane, so that you know which way the wind is blowing.

You will need

Food colouring or ink

Waterproof sticky tape

A glue stick

A short pencil with an eraser on the end
Three long pencils

A drinking straw

A shallow bowl

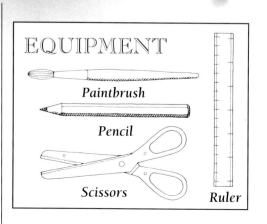

EQUIPMENT

Paintbrush

Pencil

Scissors

Ruler

A yoghurt pot

A large, straight-sided plastic bottle

Thin card

A drawing pin

Modelling clay

A narrow, clear plastic bottle*

*Use the narrowest bottle you can find.

Making the wind vane

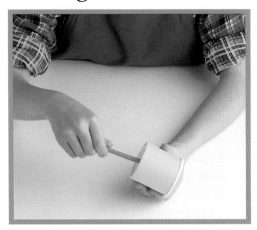

1 Make a hole in the centre of the base of the yoghurt pot. Push the short pencil into it, so the eraser end sticks out, as shown.

2 Cut four small triangles out of thin card. Then cut out a triangle about 3 cm deep and a bigger one about 5 cm deep.

3 Glue the four small triangles to the base of the yoghurt pot, so that they point in four different directions, as shown.

4 Cut 1 cm slits at both sides of each end of the straw. Slot the two big triangles into them, pointing in the same direction.

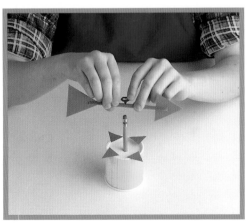

5 Push the drawing pin through the centre of the straw**. Then stick the pin into the eraser. Make sure the vane can spin easily.

6 Make a sausage of modelling clay and bend it into a ring. Push the clay around the base of the wind vane.

**Ask an adult to help you.

25

WEATHER WATCH

Making the rain gauge

1 Cut off the top quarter of the large plastic bottle, using the scissors. Ask an adult to help you make the first cut.

2 Slide the top of the bottle upside down into the base of the bottle, to act as a funnel. Tape the edges together, as shown.

3 Cut tiny strips of sticky tape. Tape them to the side of the bottle about a centimetre apart, to act as a measuring scale.

Making the barometer

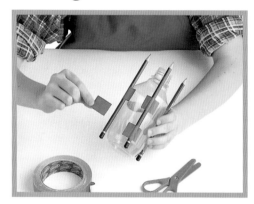

1 Tape three long pencils to the small plastic bottle. The points of the pencils should stick out above the top of the bottle.

2 Using the bottle to help you, stick three lumps of modelling clay to the bottom of the bowl, for the pencils to go into.

3 Half fill both the bowl and the bottle with water. Add a few drops of food colouring to the water with the paintbrush.

4 Cover the top of the bottle with your hand. Turn it upside-down and lower it under the water in the bowl.

5 Take your hand away from the mouth of the bottle. Keeping the bottle straight, push the pencils firmly into the modelling clay.

6 Cut tiny strips of sticky tape. Tape them to the side of the bottle to make a scale, as when making the rain gauge.

RECORDING THE WEATHER

Stand your wind vane and rain gauge outside. Keep the barometer indoors, away from direct sunlight. Check your weather station every day and make a record of any changes in a notebook. As well as reading the instruments you have made, write down how many hours of rain or sun there have been and note what sort of clouds are in the sky.

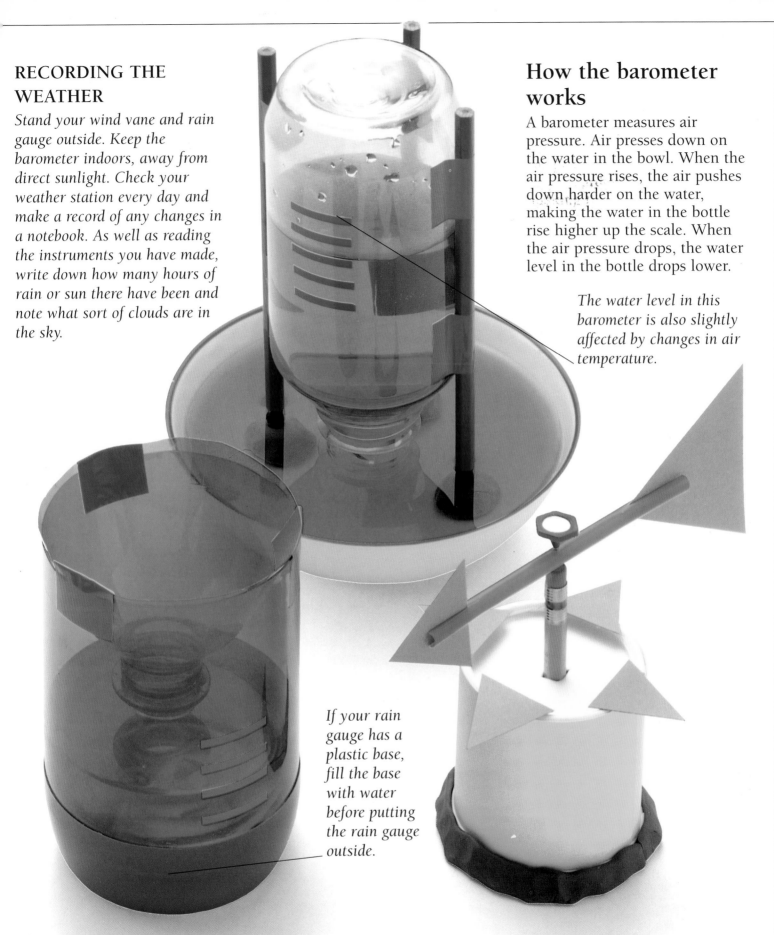

How the barometer works

A barometer measures air pressure. Air presses down on the water in the bowl. When the air pressure rises, the air pushes down harder on the water, making the water in the bottle rise higher up the scale. When the air pressure drops, the water level in the bottle drops lower.

The water level in this barometer is also slightly affected by changes in air temperature.

If your rain gauge has a plastic base, fill the base with water before putting the rain gauge outside.

Measuring the rainfall

When it rains, check how far up the scale the water comes. Make a note of the reading, then empty the rain gauge.

Which way is the wind blowing?

Stand the wind vane outside on a flat surface. Use a compass to position it so that one of the triangles points north. Mark the triangles north, south, east, and west. Write down which direction the wind is blowing from. The north wind, for example, blows from north to south.

MAKE IT MOVE !

When you look at a sequence of action photographs passing quickly before your eyes, the images look as if they are moving, just like a film at the cinema. You can see this effect by looking into a machine called a zoetrope. Before you make the zoetrope, you will need to take 13 photographs showing someone doing each stage of a simple action. Below, photographs of a clown lifting his hat and then putting it back on are used.

EQUIPMENT

Scissors

Pencil

Compass

Craft knife

Ruler

Coloured card

You will need

A sequence of 13 action photographs taken on a plain background

Jar lid

Medium-sized beads

Two empty cotton reels

Strong glue

Pencil

Coloured sticky tape

Making the zoetrope

1 Use a compass to draw a circle with a radius of 12.5 cm on card. Cut it out. Draw round a cotton reel in the circle's centre.

2 Ask an adult to cut slightly within the cotton reel circle, making a hole that the cotton reel fits into without sliding out.

3 Glue one cotton reel on to the inside of a jar lid and one to the outside. Glue a pencil into the reel on the outside of the lid.

4 Cut a strip of card 11.5 cm x 81 cm*. Measure 0.5 cm wide slots every 5.5 cm. Mark them all along one edge of the card.

5 Mark each of the 0.5 cm wide slots to be 4 cm deep. Use a ruler to draw the slots neatly. Cut them out.

6 Overlap the ends of the slotted card by 2 cm and glue them to make a tube. Tape the circle of card to the tube to make a base.

7 Trim the prints to make small rectangles and stick them on to a strip of card 7.5 cm x 80 cm**. Leave a 2 cm gap at one end.

8 Overlap the card by 2 cm and glue it to make a tube with the prints on the inside. Put the card in the drum, and beads in the jar lid.

9 Push the cotton reel through the hole in the base of the drum. It should fit snugly. The zoetrope is now ready to spin!

*You can stick two strips of card together to make it stronger. We have used yellow and blue card.

**The cut-out prints should measure 6 cm x 6 cm. Stick them down in order to make an action sequence.

THE FINISHED ZOETROPE

When you spin the drum and look through the slits, the pictures will appear to move! The drum spins on the loose beads in the jar lid. Try making several action sequences to place inside your zoetrope. You and your friends will have lots of fun seeing each other in action.

THE ZOETROPE PHOTOGRAPHS

Ask a friend to wear bright colours that will show up well and to stand against a plain background. The plain background will help you to join the photographs together easily. Take the photographs outside on a sunny day or use your camera's flash indoors.

When you glue your action photographs on to card, leave a thin border of card at the top and bottom. This will help your photographs to stand out.

Blue and yellow sheets of card were stuck together to make this zoetrope. Using two sheets makes the drum stronger.

A SIMPLE ACTION

Keep your action shots simple. Someone waving, clapping, or taking off a hat, as shown here, are easy shots to take. Get a friend to do the action very slowly and to stop at each stage so that you can take a photograph of each small move. Remember to sort the action photographs into the correct order when you get the prints.

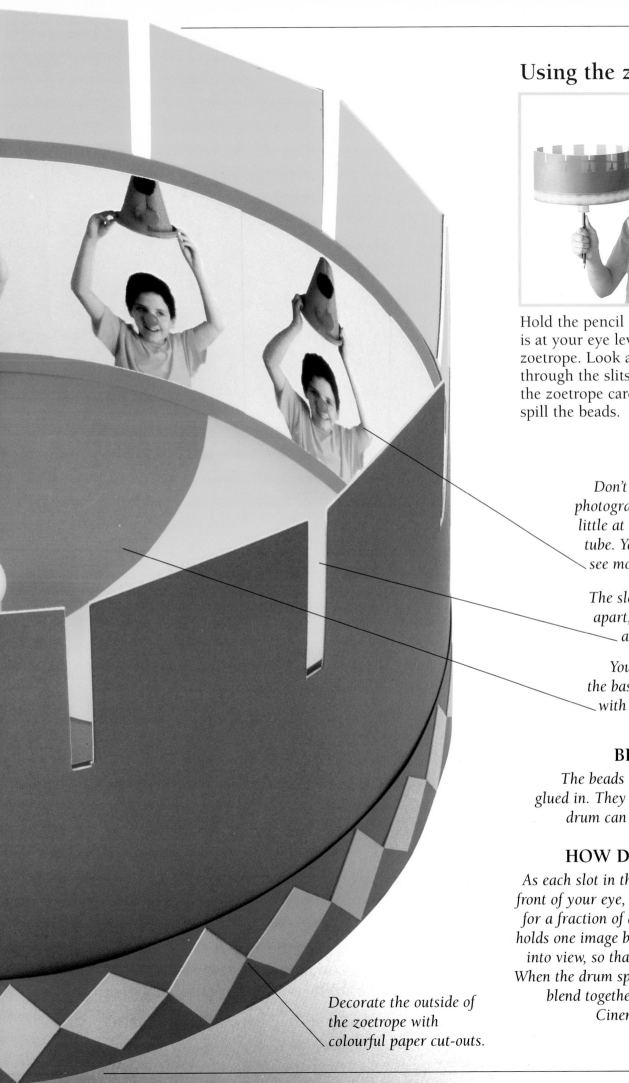

Using the zoetrope

Hold the pencil so that the drum is at your eye level. Spin the zoetrope. Look at the photographs through the slits in the drum. Hold the zoetrope carefully so you don't spill the beads.

Don't worry if your photographs overlap a little at the join of the tube. You should still see moving pictures.

The slots are 5.5 cm apart, 0.5 cm wide, and 4 cm deep.

You can decorate the base of the drum with paper shapes.

BEAD BEARINGS

The beads in the jar lid are not glued in. They are loose so that the drum can spin round on them.

HOW DOES IT WORK?

As each slot in the zoetrope passes in front of your eye, you see each picture for a fraction of a second. Your brain holds one image before the next comes into view, so that the pictures merge. When the drum spins fast, the pictures blend together and seem to move. Cinema film works in the same way.

Decorate the outside of the zoetrope with colourful paper cut-outs.

31